The Great Monologues
from the
Mark Taper Forum

Smith and Kraus *Books For Actors*
THE MONOLOGUE SERIES
The Best Men's/Women's Stage Monologues of 1993
The Best Men's/Women's Stage Monologues of 1992
The Best Men's/Women's Stage Monologues of 1991
The Best Men's/Women's Stage Monologues of 1990
One Hundred Men's/Women's Stage Monologues from the 1980's
2 Minutes and Under: Character Monologues for Actors
Street Talk: Character Monologues for Actors
Uptown: Character Monologues for Actors
Monologues from Contemporary Literature: Volume I
Monologues from Classic Plays
FESTIVAL MONOLOGUE SERIES
The Great Monologues from the Humana Festival
The Great Monologues from the EST Marathon
The Great Monologues from the Women's Project
YOUNG ACTORS SERIES
Great Scenes and Monologues for Children
New Plays from A.C.T.'s Young Conservatory
Great Scenes for Young Actors from the Stage
Great Monologues for Young Actors
Multicultural Monologues for Young Actors
Multicultural Scenes for Young Actors
SCENE STUDY SERIES
Scenes From Classic Plays 468 B.C. to 1960 A.D.
The Best Stage Scenes of 1993
The Best Stage Scenes of 1992
The Best Stage Scenes for Women from the 1980's
The Best Stage Scenes for Men from the 1980's
CONTEMPORARY PLAYWRIGHTS
Romulus Linney: 17 Short Plays
Eric Overmyer: Collected Plays
Lanford Wilson: 21 Short Plays
William Mastrosimone: Collected Plays
Horton Foote: 4 New Plays
Terrence McNally: 15 Short Plays
Women Playwrights: The Best Plays of 1992
Humana Festival '93: The Complete Plays
Women Playwrights: The Best Plays of 1993
GREAT TRANSLATION FOR ACTORS SERIES
The Wood Demon: Anton Chekhov *translated by N. Saunders & F. Dwyer*
The Seagull: Anton Chekhov *translated by N. Saunders & F. Dwyer*
Three Sisters: Anton Chekhov *translated by Lanford Wilson*
OTHER BOOKS IN OUR COLLECTION
The Actor's Chekhov
Kiss and Tell: Restoration Scenes, Monologues, & History
Cold Readings: Some Do's and Don'ts for Actors at Auditions

If you require pre-publication information about upcoming Smith and Kraus monologue collections, scene collections, play anthologies, advanced acting books, and
books for young actors, you may receive our semi-annual catalogue, free of charge, by
sending your name and address to *Smith and Kraus Catalogue, P.O. Box 127 One
Main Street, Lyme, NH 03768 phone 1-800-862-5423, fax 1-603-795-4427.*

The Great Monologues
from the
Mark Taper Forum

edited by Kristin Graham

Festival Monologue Series

S&K
A Smith and Kraus Book

Published by Smith and Kraus, Inc.
Newbury, Vermont
Copyright © 1994 by Smith and Kraus, Inc.
All rights reserved

COVER AND TEXT DESIGN BY JULIA HILL
Manufactured in the United States of America

First Edition: May 1994
10 9 8 7 6 5 4 3 2 1

NOTE: These monologues are intended to be used for audition and class study; permission is not required to use the material for those purposes. However, if there is a paid performance of any of the monologues included in this book, please refer to the permissions acknowledgment pages to locate the source who can grant permission for public performance.

Library of Congress Cataloging-in-Publication Data
The Great monologues from the Mark Taper Forum / edited by Kristen Graham. --
1st ed.
       p.   cm. --(Monologue audition series)
       ISBN 1-880399-13-X : $7.95
       1. Acting. 2. Monologues. 3. American drama. I. Graham,
Kristin. II. Mark Taper Forum (Los Angeles, Calif.) III. Series.
       PN2080.G7215   1994
       812'.04508--dc20   94-10072
                                          CIP

Contents

Introduction

The Mark Taper Forum has been a place of artistic diversity and freedom from the moment we came together in 1967. Our first play, THE DEVILS, caused such furor that some members of the Los Angeles theater–going community tried to close us down. But this crucible helped form our identity as a theater. Over the last twenty–seven years, we have continued to provide a home for a wide array of artists, both American and international, and to challenge our audiences with new worlds, new ways of thinking, new journeys.

When people think of our theater, they see our mainstage with its characteristic thrust. But, as you will see in this volume, the Taper is also a laboratory for new work. Over the years, we have produced a second stage, a literary cabaret space, and various festivals and special programs devoted to the furtherance of contemporary plays by young and established writers. This book provides you with a cross–section of our work, spanning four decades. Some, such as THE SHADOW BOX and THE KENTUCKY CYCLE, have become signature plays and are internationally representative of the kind of work we do on our mainstage. Others are more the kind of cutting edge work which explodes and empowers and suggests new kinds of writing for the theater. Some have been fully produced, some have travelled to other theaters and have entered the repertoire of American theater and some are still waiting for production somewhere. All together, they create a full and up–to–the–moment picture of what has happened and keeps happening at the Taper.

Two good things happen when you read these short pieces. First, you become familiar with new plays, which hopefully will propel you to actually go and read them, the whole play, and thereby understand the monologue in context, and perhaps find a way to give life to the entire play in your work. Second, there is an undeniable power in using new material for audition purposes. When you enter an audition with an unexpected and fresh monologue, you immediately help the auditioner listen with fresh ears and he or she is more likely to remember you, which is, of course, a very good thing.

One other comment. The Taper has always been a home for actors. My respect and love for the acting profession remains total—and usually begins when something alive, original and truthful emerges in an audition. These monologues are markers along the road of our ongoing journey in the American theater, and all of us are a part of the experience.

—*Gordon Davidson, Artistic Director, Mark Taper Forum*

The Great Monologues
from the
Mark Taper Forum

AN AMERICAN COMEDY
Richard Nelson

Set in the 1930s, *An American Comedy* takes place aboard an ocean-liner in a first-class cabin. One partner of a successful playwrighting team has reacted to the Depression by becoming a Communist who only wants to write serious plays with a message.

Here, George, the other half of the team, tells his agent that he was once as idealistic as Max, until an incident opened his eyes to his true character.

♦ ♦ ♦

GEORGE: I once had this friend. He was a writer. And like Max, he started thinking about everything that's wrong in the world.

[**JOE:** For a writer that is death.]

GEORGE: [I know that.] And just like Max, he began reading all those leftist books and newspapers, and he started going to meetings, then he was speaking at these meetings, and pretty soon he had all these ideas about society and poor people and things like that. And like Max, he wasn't content just to have these ideas, he would not stop until he had put these ideas into his writing.

[**JOE:** Some people just don't know when to stop!]

GEORGE: Suddenly the whole world was his cause. He was full of convictions, and prided himself on his social awareness. (*Beat.*) But then, Joe, something happened. One day he and his wife were on the subway and who should sit next to his wife but a colored man. Of course, he didn't think anything about it.

[**JOE:** Those animals.]

GEORGE: And then it happened. Call it protecting one's loved one. Call it irrational fear. Call it whatever you want, but, my friend found himself standing in the middle of the car screaming at this man. (*Beat.*) Pretty soon the rest of the car was screaming at him too. And a few minutes later, two cops came by, and my friend remembers watching this poor colored man being pulled off the train at 72nd Street and he remembers thinking – wasn't this the very same kind of person he'd so much wanted to help? (*Beat.*) He was shocked with himself. And it was then that he realized he was no social reformer. And not a day has gone by since then, Joe, that my friend has not thanked that colored man for opening his eyes and letting him see the errors of his ways.

(*Short pause.*)

[**JOE:** That's beautiful.]

GEORGE: Of course, he had a slight relapse after hearing from the colored man's lawyer that the Negro had had a cinder in his eye. So that's why he was winking. (*Beat.*) But my friend soon realized there was no going back.

[**JOE:** Sure. It's important to stick to your convictions. Who was this friend, George? Do I know him?]

(*Short pause.*)

GEORGE: He was me.

THE BEAR FACTS
Jo Carson

Set in the 1830's in the West Tennessee woods, Davy Crockett shoots and wounds his 100th bear which sets off the magic. The bear begins to transform into a woman, is able to speak and seeks revenge for her imminent death and the death of the bears before her. A variety of characters interact and are affected by both Crockett and the bear: John Blackhawk, a lawyer running for congress against Crockett; White Elizabeth, Crockett's wife; Red Elizabeth, a Cherokee woman, and Black Elizabeth, a slave.

Indian Elizabeth, distraught at the prospect of being forced to leave her tribal land and move West, decides to impersonate a white woman in order to stay.

♦   ♦   ♦

INDIAN ELIZABETH: Who are they to say we have to move? What right have they? For land, always for more land. They eat land, and the men grow bushes on their chins for the trees they cut. Then they say, "sell us this now, we live here anyway." Sell it? How can a person sell land?

The land should sell them. The land should shake them off. It can eat them if it wants to. The land can make mouths anywhere it wants them. Sometimes I try to remind the land of its strength. I go out by myself and speak into the winds. I say, "Now would be a good time." I am afraid so many trees are gone that the winds just run straight to the edge of the world and fall off.

Where do they all come from? How can their women bear so many babies and live through it? I have wondered. I think it is because the land is rich and it has grown a crop of weeds. They do look alike. All pale like ghosts.

And now, the chief of them, Andrew, says people with red skin will have to move. I have asked what the name Andrew means and no one knows. It means nothing. They give names to one another that mean nothing. No wonder there are so many of them, their names take up no space.

Andrew Means Nothing says we have to move.

3

I cannot think of myself somewhere else. My feet have made roots. Move. Tell a tree of as many years as I have to move. Everyone would laugh at you and say you are dim–witted.

But no one is laughing at Andrew. I am scared.

I have been dreaming of a shape changer, and it has told me what to do.

I will dress like a white woman in a gown that makes my waist little and my breasts large, and they will not see my color. I will take a white name. I will be Elizabeth Means Nothing, and they will not hear my real name, and they will not know me, and I will act white, I will do like they do, and they will not remember that a woman different from them was ever here, and they will not tear my feet from their roots.

It is what I can think to do.

THE BEAR FACTS
Jo Carson

Set in the 1830's in the West Tennessee woods, Davy Crockett shoots and wounds his 100th bear which sets off the magic. The bear begins to transform into a woman, is able to speak and seeks revenge for her imminent death and the death of the bears before her. A variety of characters interact and are affected by both Crockett and the bear: John Blackhawk, a lawyer running for congress against Crockett; White Elizabeth, Crockett's wife; Red Elizabeth, a Cherokee woman, and Black Elizabeth, a slave.

Davy Crockett describes his technique for hunting bear.

♦   ♦   ♦

DAVY CROCKETT: Best bear bait in the world is a woman on the rag. It ain't the woman, it is the blood. It's wise blood, regular blood don't work as well, but there ain't a bear in the world that don't like wise blood. I tell you, they want to sleep in it. Next best bait is fresh cow meat, but seems to me, if you're going to slaughter a cow, you might as well eat it and not worry about the bear. You can burn honey in the wind, that calls 'em in. There is the problem of the bear smelling you. The solution is fox pee which ain't perfume, take my word for it, not to mention the problems of collecting it. Squeezing the pee out of foxes is a morning's work for a strong man, all by itself.

Or, you can stand in the woods and announce you are David Crockett, you are not going home without a bear, and see who volunteers.

BURN THIS
Lanford Wilson

Burn This is a story of two lonely people with little in common who are, nevertheless, irresistably drawn to each other. Anna, a dancer who is still grieving a month after the death of her roommate, a gay dancer, opens the door to Pale, her roommate Robbie's older brother. Pale, eccentric, explosive and passionate, touches Anna in ways she has never felt before and they begin an unconventional affair.

Anna has returned from out of town where she attended Robbie's funeral and met his family. Here, she describes the experience to her friend, Larry.

◆　◆　◆

ANNA: No, I should have come with you. God. Just as I think I'm out of there, some relatives drive me back to the house. The place is mobbed. I'm dragged through everybody eating and drinking and talking, to some little back bedroom, with all the aunts and cousins, with the women, right? Squashed into this room. His mother's on the bed with a washcloth on her forehead. I'm trying to tell them how I've got to get a bus back to civilization.

[**LARRY:** This is very moving, but I'm double-parked.]

[**ANNA:** Exactly.]

[**LARRY:** This is a wake?]

ANNA: [I couldn't tell you what is was, Larry, I guess.] In about eight seconds I know they have no idea that Robbie's gay.

[**LARRY:** I could have told you that.]

ANNA: They've never heard of Dom. God, I'm making up stories, I'm racking my brain for every interesting thing anyone I know has done to tell them Robbie did it. Wonderful workaholic Robbie, and I couldn't tell them a thing about him. It was all just so massively sad.

[**LARRY:** Oh, Lord.]

ANNA: It gets worse, it gets much worse. And they never saw him dance! I couldn't believe it. All the men are gorgeous, of course. They all look exactly like Robbie except in that kind of

6

blue-collar, working-at-the-steel-mill kind of way, and drink? God, could they knock it back. So then it's midnight and the last bus has left at ten, which they knew, I'm sure, damn them, and I hadn't checked, like an idiot. So I have to spend the night in Robbie's little nephew's room in the attic. The little redhead, did you see him?

[**LARRY:** I didn't see him.]

ANNA: He's been collecting butterflies all day, and they're pinned around the room to the walls – a pin in each wing, right?

[**LARRY:** I'm not liking this little redheaded nephew.]

ANNA: Darling, wait. So I get to sleep by about two, I've got them to promise to get me up at six-thirty for the seven-something bus. I wake up, it's not quite light, really; you can't see in the room much – but there's something in there.

[**LARRY:** Oh, God.]

ANNA: There's this intermittent soft flutter sound. I think what the hell is – Larry, the – oh, Lord, the walls are just pulsating. All those butterflies are alive. They're all beating their bodies against the walls – all around me. The kid's put them in alcohol; he thought he'd killed them, they'd only passed out.

[**LARRY:** Oh, God.]

ANNA: I started screaming hysterically. I got the bedsheet around me, ran down to the kitchen; I've never felt so naked in my life. Of course I was naked – a sheet wrapped around me. This glowering older brother had to go get my clothes, unpinned the butterflies, who knows if they lived. I got the whispering sister –

[**LARRY:** What a family.]

ANNA: – to drop me off at the bus station; they were glad to get rid of me. I was an hour and a half early, I didn't care. I drank about twenty cups of that vending-machine coffee. Black; the cream and sugar buttons didn't work. The bus-station attendant is ogling me. I'm so wired from the caffeine, if he'd said anything I'd have kneecapped him. There's these two bag ladies yelling at each other, apparently they're rivals. I fit right in.

BURN THIS
Lanford Wilson

Burn This is a story of two lonely people with little in common who are, nevertheless, irresistably drawn to each other. Anna, a dancer who is still grieving a month after the death of her roommate, a gay dancer, opens the door to Pale, her roommate Robbie's older brother. Pale, eccentric, explosive and passionate, touches Anna in ways she has never felt before and they begin an unconventional affair.

Pale shows up at Anna's loft at midnight to collect Robbie's things. Talking non-stop he complains about a guy who talks too much and people who don't listen.

♦   ♦   ♦

[**ANNA:** What did you do to your hand?]

[**PALE:** No, this bar tonight, Ray, you know?]

[**ANNA:** Good ol' Ray, sure. I mean, we've only talked on the phone.]

PALE: Anybody needs relieving. I'm a roving fireman. Very healthy occupation. I'm puttin' out somebody else's fire. I'm puttin' out my own. *Quid pro* – something; symbiosis. Or sometimes you just let it burn. (*Pause.*)

There was this character runnin' off at the mouth; I told him I'm gonna push his face in, he don't shut up. Now, this should be a fairly obvious statement, right? But this dipshit starts trying to explain to me what he's been saying *ad nauseam* all night, like there was some subtle gradation of thought that was gonna make it all right that he was mouthing this horseshit. So when I'm forced to bust the son of a bitch, he's down on the floor, he's dripping blood from a split lip, he's testing a loose tooth, and that fucker is *still talking*. Now, some people might think that this was the problem of this guy, he's got this motor going, he's not privy to where the shutoff valve is. But I gotta come to the conclusion that I'm weird. Cause I try to communicate with these jerkoffs in what is *essentially* the mother tongue, but no one is picking me up; they're not reading me. There's some mystery here. Okay, sometimes they're just on a rap. I respect rap. You're not supposed to be listening. You can read the paper, watch TV, eat pistachios, I'm not talking that. I'm talking these jerkoffs think you're listening. [You said the choreographer organizes what? Sculptured space? What is that?]

[**ANNA:** Oh, God. I'm sorry – What did you say? I'm sorry.]

[**PALE:** Now, see, that I can't take. I can't stand that.]

[**ANNA:** I'm sorry, really, but –]

PALE: Well, see, fine, you got these little social phrases and politenesses – all they show me is this – like – giganticness of unconcern with your "I'm sorrys," man. The fuckin' world is going down the fuckin' toilet on "I'm sorrys." I'm sorry is this roll of toilet paper – they're growing whole forests, for people to wipe their asses on with their "I'm sorrys." Be a tree. For one day. And know that that tree over there is gonna be maybe music paper, the Boss is gonna make forty million writin' some poor-slob-can't-get work song on. This tree is gonna be ten-dollar bills, get passed around, buy things, *mean something*, hear stories; we got sketch pads and fuckin' "I don't love you anymore" letters pinned to some creep's pillow – something of *import*. Headlines, box scores, some great book or movie script – Jack Nicholson's gonna mark you all up, say whatever he wishes to, anyway, out in some fuckin' desert, you're supposed to be his *text*, he's gonna lay out this line of coke on you – Tree over there is gonna be some four-star restaurant, they're gonna call him parchment, bake pompano in him. And you're stuck in the ground, you can't go nowhere, all you know is some fuckin' junkie's gonna wipe his ass and flush you down the East River. Go floating out past the Statue of Liberty all limp and covered with shit, get tangled up in some Saudi Arabian oil tanker's fuckin' propellers – you got maybe three hundred years before you drift down to Brazil somewhere and get a chance to be maybe a coffee bush. "I'm sorrys" are fuck, man.

BURN THIS
Lanford Wilson

Burn This is a story of two lonely people with little in common who are, nevertheless, irresistably drawn to each other. Anna, a dancer who is still grieving a month after the death of her roommate, a gay dancer, opens the door to Pale, her roommate Robbie's older brother. Pale, eccentric, explosive and passionate, touches Anna in ways she has never felt before and they begin an unconventional affair.

Pale, still talking incessantly, tells Anna what turns him on.

◆   ◆   ◆

PALE: I like a lot of things. You want bullshit, you want to know what turns me on?

[**ANNA:** Nothing. That's fine. I can imagine.]

PALE: [Yeah, well, I don't like being imagined.] I like the ocean. That hurricane. I stayed on the pier – hanging on to this fuckin' pipe railing, wind blowin' so hard you couldn't breathe. Couldn't open my hands the next day. Try to get excited over some fuckin' roller coaster, some loop-the-loop after that. I like those gigantic, citywide fires – like Passaic, wherever; fuckin' Jersey's burnin' down three times a week. Good riddance. Avalanches! Whole villages wiped out. Somethin' that can – like – amaze you. People don't want to hear that shit, they want-like you should get turned on by some crap – you know, Häagen-Dazs ice cream, "I like everyone to be nice." That shit. Chicks or somethin'. Gettin' laid's okay. A really hot shower's good. Clean underwear, smells like Downy softener. (*Beat.*) So you guys all cook for each other. Sittin' here, makin' polite conversation about the state of the world and shit.

THE DISTANCE OF YOU
Adelaide MacKenzie

The Distance of You is set in three houses, side-by-side in a Canyon in the desolate, smog-filled landscape of L.A. All the characters living close to each other are emotionally dysfunctional and all are either searching for something or running *from* something. Suna, who seems to be trying to escape from something, is restless and dissatisfied. She is staying with her friend, Satu, who plans parties for guests who never come, and both buy cocaine from a neighbor, Reed, who has a crush on Satu. Petra, the middle neighbor, spends most of the play jealously watching Reed through the window as he interacts with Suna and Satu. In the third house live an ailing, controlling mother; her "good," compliant daughter, Beth, and the "black sheep," Jessica. She has recently returned home, hoping to convince Beth to leave with her and her boyfriend, Ted, or at the very least, get some money.

Suna, 25-30, tells her friend Satu about a girl she is jealous of and how she would like to deal with her.

◆　◆　◆

SUNA: She always wears yellow bikinis.
  She has one of those skinny poochy
  little girl tummies.
  And they all stare at her.
  The wall – of the pool –
  It's an Olympic size pool,
  Tiled.
  Beautiful.
  Sometimes it's empty.
  It's just me and Nancy.
  Side by side.
  When she swims next to me –
  Ignoring me –
  I hate to be ignored, Satu.
[**SATU:** Nobody likes it.
  Maybe the video stores aren't even open.
  Because of the tremor.]
SUNA: Like I don't count.

11

Because I'm not a guy.
Fuck her.
(*Silence.*)
One day I'm going to grab her head
And pound
And keep pounding
Pounding
Pounding
Right on the wall there
Just keep pounding
On the side –
The temple –
Pounding
Until it opens up.

THE DISTANCE OF YOU
Adelaide MacKenzie

The Distance of You is set in three houses, side-by-side in a Canyon in the desolate, smog-filled landscape of L.A. All the characters living close to each other are emotionally dysfunctional and all are either searching for something or running *from* something. Suna, who seems to be trying to escape from something, is restless and dissatisfied. She is staying with her friend, Satu, who plans parties for guests who never come, and both buy cocaine from a neighbor, Reed, who has a crush on Satu. Petra, the middle neighbor, spends most of the play jealously watching Reed through the window as he interacts with Suna and Satu. In the third house live an ailing, controlling mother; her "good," compliant daughter, Beth, and the "black sheep," Jessica. She has recently returned home, hoping to convince Beth to leave with her and her boyfriend, Ted, or at the very least, get some money.

Lieutenant Halsey, an Arizona police officer (over 40), unexpectedly arrives at Satu's house, much to the consternation of Suna, who seems to want to avoid him. Lt. Halsey claims to be friends with Joe Wambaugh, a former LAPD cop, now a successful novelist and screenwriter. It becomes clear that Suna has killed someone in Arizona and that Lt. Halsey was the arresting officer. He has become obsessed with Suna and has pursued her, not to arrest her, but to possess her. Here, he makes it clear that he wants to make her live with him and become totally dependent on him.

♦   ♦   ♦

LIEUTENANT HALSEY: Friends are important. They can save
   your life. (*Pause.*) If I was going to
   write a book – and I might – because
   I know Joe – He could give me tips –
   I'd – ahh – portray the world in a way –
   I'd show something – that –
   Well – I'd call it THE CONFESSOR.
[**SUNA**: I'll do the dishes now.]
   (*Suna gets up. Lieutenant pulls her down roughly.*)
LIEUTENANT HALSEY: It's all about – it goes like this –
   You can lie to everybody in the world.
   You can deceive.

You can be deceived.
And then one day there is only one person left.
There is only one person you have not betrayed.
And that one person – is your god.
They will be a god for you.
Because – this is why –
They only know you as good.
And that's the person you call.
In the end.

THE DISTANCE OF YOU
Adelaide MacKenzie

The Distance of You is set in three houses, side-by-side in a Canyon in the desolate, smog-filled landscape of L.A. All the characters living close to each other are emotionally dysfunctional and all are either searching for something or running *from* something. Suna, who seems to be trying to escape from something, is restless and dissatisfied. She is staying with her friend, Satu, who plans parties for guests who never come, and both buy cocaine from a neighbor, Reed, who has a crush on Satu. Petra, the middle neighbor, spends most of the play jealously watching Reed through the window as he interacts with Suna and Satu. In the third house live an ailing, controlling mother; her "good," compliant daughter, Beth, and the "black sheep," Jessica. She has recently returned home, hoping to convince Beth to leave with her and her boyfriend, Ted, or at the very least, get some money.

Alone, Petra angrily denounces Reed, condemning her own obsession with him.

◆   ◆   ◆

(*Petra holding binoculars. She slams them down. Furious.*)
PETRA: That's it.
    You're a fuck up!
    That's all there is to it.
    I don't love you anymore anyway.
    You bore me.
    All of this bores me.
    And her tits are fake – by the way.
    She wants you for your drugs.
    That's clear.
    So what.
    Big deal.
    It didn't work out.
    I'm going to kill myself over you?
    No way.
    I'm moving on.
    There are other guys.
    There are other canyons.

You're a jerk, Reed.
(*Pause.*)
If I really cared I'd kill you.
But I don't.
I don't even care
Because I don't love you anymore.
I've changed my mind.
And that's a woman's prerogative.

THE DREAM COAST
John Steppling

The Dream Coast is a portrait of a group of misfits and losers on the fringes of society in L.A. Most are on various drugs.

Lana, 40, is married to Drew, a fringe criminal and "trouble-shooter" for Wilson, owner of their apartment building. While smoking a joint, Lana confides to Marliss, an addict who turns tricks for drug money, how she always wanted to have a baby.

♦   ♦   ♦

LANA: I've been pregnant – one time, and had the abortion. Wasn't Drew. But it's funny because I tried and tried for so long to have a baby, and I'd cry myself to sleep, all alone, not having one, and I prayed . . . which is funny, too . . . and I'd look down at my body, in bed, I'd be on my back and I'd look at myself through one of those skimpy nighties I wore, and I saw myself, really saw – this *is* what I'd see with my eyes, was a greenish bark, my flesh turned to a hard tree bark, like a fuckin' tree stump with green legs . . . (*Pause.*) Lying there, with very pale light, coming from somewhere, and it'd make me cry more, and I'd get afraid to move, and I'd get afraid to move, as if this dead tree trunk there, with this thick tough bark, in the winter light would move, as part of me, we'd move and that would be it, that would be the whole story, the end of all things. . . (*Trails off into a hoarse distant laugh which in turn becomes a brutal coughing fit. Silence. Lights out.*)

DREAM ON MONKEY MOUNTAIN:
TI-JEAN AND HIS BROTHERS
Derek Walcott

Monkey Mountain is an anthology of plays written about and first produced in the West Indies.

Ti-Jean and His Brothers is a fable about Bolom, a still-born, misshapen, child-demon who hates all mothers and jealously wants to kill their sons. He challenges three brothers to make him feel human emotions which is the only thing that will make him human. In return he promises unlimited wealth, fulfillment, and peace. Ultimately, Ti-Jean, the youngest, wins the bet when he makes the demon feel sorrow.

Gros-Jean, the eldest, describes a bet he made with a white planter (the devil in disguise) as to who could lose his temper first.

♦   ♦   ♦

GROS-JEAN: (*In another part of the wood.*) I have an arm of iron, and that's true, but I here since the last two days working for this damn white man, and I don't give a damn if he watching me. You know what I doing here with this bag and this piece of stick? Well, I go tell you. While I smoke a pipe. Let me just sit down, and I won't lose my patience. (*He sits on a log.*) Well, you remember how I leave home, and then bounce up this old man who put me on to a work? Remember what the old son of a leaf-gathering beggar said? He said that working for the Devil was the shortest way to success. Well, I walked up through the bush then I come onto a large field. Estate-like, you know. Sugar, tobacco, and a hell of a big white house where they say the Devil lives. Ay-ay.

So two next black fellers bring me up to him. Big white man, his hand cold as an axe blade and his mind twice as sharp. So he say, "Gros-Jean, we has a deal to make, right?" So I say, "Sure, boss!" He say the one that get the other one vex, the one who show the first sign of anger will be eaten rrruuunnnhhh, just like that, right? You think I stupid? I strong, I have some sense and my name not Gros-Jean for nothing. That was two days ago. Well, Jesus, a man ain't rest since then! The first job I had was to stand up in a sugar-cane field and count all the leaves of the cane. That take me up till four o'clock. I count all the leaves and then divide by the number of stalks. I must tell you there had times when I was getting vex but the old iron arm fix me, because there is patience in strength. The Devil ain't say anything. About seven o'clock, he tell me to go and catch about seventy fireflies. Well, you must try and catch fireflies! Is not easy. Had a time when I do so once, one whap with the hand! Thinking was a bunch but was nothing, only stars! So in the middle of all that, this man come up to me and say, "What's the matter, Joe," he always like he don't know my name, but I is me, Gros-Jean, the strongest! And if you ain't know my name, you best don't call me nothing. Say, "What's matter, Mac? You vex or sumpin?" So I say, "No, I ain't vex!" Well, is two days now, and I ain't get a cent. I so tired I giddy. But I giving the old iron arm a rest from cramp, and breaking a little smoke. After all! If was only sensible work, if a man could get the work that suit him, cotton or sugar or something important! Plus he getting eighty-five per cent of the profit? Shucks, man, that ain't fair. Besides I could just bust his face, you know. But me mother ain't bring me up so. After all, man, after all, a man have to rest man. Shime!

DREAM ON MONKEY MOUNTAIN:
THE SEA AT DAUPHIN
Derek Walcott

Monkey Mountain is an anthology of plays written about and first produced in the West Indies.

The Sea at Dauphin chronicles the difficult life of fishermen in the West Indies. Afa, over 40, is described as "gritty-tempered."

Afa explains why he must live and die by the harshness and beauty of the sea.

♦ ♦ ♦

AFA: This brave I have it come from many years,
Many years of sea, many years dolour.
That crack my face, and make my heart so hard.
If none going, then I will go alone.
If I don't have no love I don't have hate,
If I don't have woman, there is sea and sky.
God is a white man. The sky is his blue eye,
His spit on Dauphin people is the sea.
Don't ask me why a man must work so hard
To eat for worm to get more fat. Maybe I bewitch.
You never curse God, I curse him, and cannot die,
Until His time. This basin men call sea
Never get red for men blood it have. My turn is next.
I cannot sleep on land, like Gacia.
The land is hard, this Dauphin land have stone
Where it should have some heart. The sea
It have compassion in the end.

DREAM ON MONKEY MOUNTAIN:
THE SEA AT DAUPHIN
Derek Walcott

Monkey Mountain is an anthology of plays written about and first produced in the West Indies.

The Sea at Dauphin chronicles the difficult life of fishermen in the West Indies. Afa, over 40, is described as "gritty-tempered."

Afa describes the death of Bolo, an old fisherman.

◆　　◆　　◆

AFA: And Augustin have half a bonito for the old man, and so we go up the *ajoupa* on the hill by Dauphin side. And he not there, is only his woman grave. And the garden dead, the old corn dying standing up and the yellow dog is hungry. And Augustin wrap the fish, half a bonito, and put it on top the house and a banana leaf to mark it. And coming down the hill just now we hear the woman singing, and I look at Agos and he look at me afraid. And we meet Debel drunk looking for us and Debel say this morning he see him sitting on the sand and counting bird. (*Takes a drink.*) And this afternoon Debel come back, was to catch crab, and he is not there, only the wood-trees and the sand blowing . . . And Debel say he look for him and meet a old man was driving goat from dry grass, and say he see him climbing on the high rocks by where they have the statue of Sainte Vierge . . . And this afternoon they had a boy was fishing for whelks under La Vierge by Maingot side, and see this thing, and the boy turn it over on the sand with his foot, and when they look is him. And the fish on top his house is rotten, faster than old man is dead . . .

[**WOMAN'S VOICE:** Gacia! Gacia!]

[**GACIA:** Alors?]

AFA: (*Looking to sea.*) Last year Annelles, and Bolo, and this year Hounakin . . . And one day, tomorrow, you Gacia, and me . . . And Augustin . . . And we have only this shell for his old woman is in the *cimetière* behind the church, where Fond

River coming down by the canes and making one with the sea at Dauphin . . .

HELLS KITCHEN ABLAZE
Thomas George Carter

Set in an abandoned warehouse, eight flights up, *Hells Kitchen Ablaze*, is a powerful and disturbing look at the lives of eight N.Y.P.D. cops in the Narcotics division. These tough, street-wise cops have a camaraderie, loyalty, and ruthlessness akin to the Mafia or the street gangs they are supposed to be fighting. It is learned that one of their friends was killed during a bad drug bust and that another cop shot and killed a young boy in an alley, by mistake. It is also revealed that these cops are "on the take," waiting in this warehouse for a large sum of money from a Colombian drug lord. When three of the cops – L'Arena, Fontagredda, and Mishkeno – discover that the others are working undercover for the DEA, the three execute them with a bullet behind the ear.

Camagitello is a cop working undercover for the DEA in hopes of getting off for shooting the kid by mistake. Here he describes what happened that night to his fellow officers.

♦   ♦   ♦

CAMAGITELLO: When I was a kid, in Brooklyn. I used to play in alleys. Alleys used to be paradise. But, ya can't play no more in alleys, 'cause the pushers an' the junkies run the alleys. (*Beat.*) I know 'ez in there, this dealer I'm chasin'. It's dark. Pile'a trash falls over on toppa me . . . I think I see a gun . . . I unload . . . kill a kid   . . . who's hidin' in it. Stugatz dealer, he jumps the fence.   I . . . hold 'em in my arms, rock 'em, he . . . 'ez seven . . . but he weighs a thou'zan tons to me . . . I wanna give most my cut to the kid's mom. I'll be careful, she won't know where she goddit from . . . I'm gettin' phone calls at home. At home! My kids hadda change school twice a'ready. My oldest daughter, Domonique, fifteen, she lost her cheerleadin' spot, hadda give it to a nigger. My Anna Marie, she won't make love to me, 'cause I shot a nigger. The nigger community's up in arms, so the department decides they're gonna cut my ass off, give me up . . . slowly, but surely. You watch. They do it slow. My . . . wife, 'n my kids are my life, this is my job—they're my life. Not this . . . Mook pusher gits away. The fence is still shakin'. Fuck it. I got . . . fuckin' niggers callin' me at home. I can't even gidduh hard on. Niggers. Harrassin' my—Niggers—Risk my—Niggers—I risk my balls to save their asses—Niggers from destruction that they're bent on—they're—'Ey—if anybody's balls out on geno-fuckin'–side —it's niggers. FUCK 'UM. FUCK 'UM. I'm keepin' my cut. Whole. Unadulterated.

THE INTERPRETER OF HORROR
Kelly Stuart

Set in a tacky, coffee shop, *The Interpreter of Horror* pits Alan, a frustrated, dictatorial manager, against a disrespectful and macabre waitress who calls herself, "Horror." Horror reads about gruesome murders, incessantly, seeing them as a metaphor for her life. When June, a sweet, young and slightly neurotic woman, is hired as a second waitress, a struggle ensues between the uptight manager and Horror for control over the hapless June.

June's ex-boyfriend attempts to fix her up with Frank, a well-meaning but bland teacher who is determined to go out with June. Here, June describes an incident to Frank that explains how her destructive pattern in relationships began.

♦ ♦ ♦

JUNE: You know, I grew up in the valley. And I'll tell you, I'm sorry that this was the place I grew up because there's nothing there.

This guy took me once to Laserium. We went to Laserium together. That was our date.

I remember being up in Griffifth Park looking down at the lights. I remember this guy had a white suit jacket. People were into disco then and he dressed like that, like some disco guy. He wanted to take me dancing he said. He started to kiss me. It gave me this feeling of desolation. I had gotten really drunk, in fact, it was the first time I ever drank and I was determined to drink it all.

To drink whatever this disco guy bought me. I thought I should be so grateful for the tickets, the expensive tickets to Laserium and grateful for the money he spent on gas and grateful for the beer, so I kissed this guy because he was a nice guy.

But after I did, right after we kissed, I threw up. I did and I threw up a lot and I wanted to crawl down the hillside and lay there. I wanted to lay there the rest of my life.

He said get in my van and I'll take you home. We were miles and miles from the valley. I knew it was going to be a long drive and I felt desolate. Then that's it. I never saw this guy again.

He called me but when I answered the phone I said "Oh June . . . She isn't here. She'll be back soon. Do you want her to call?" And he said yes but I knew that he knew. He knew it was me. He called one more time and then, that was it. He was very friendly. He just asked for June. And that was it.

THE INTERPRETER OF HORROR
Kelly Stuart

Set in a tacky, coffee shop, *The Interpreter of Horror* pits Alan, a frustrated, dictatorial manager, against a disrespectful and macabre waitress who calls herself, "Horror." Horror reads about gruesome murders, incessantly, seeing them as a metaphor for her life. When June, a sweet, young and slightly neurotic woman, is hired as a second waitress, a struggle ensues between the uptight manager and Horror for control over the hapless June.

Horror relates a story to June meant to warn June against being lulled into becoming a victim.

♦   ♦   ♦

HORROR: I used to work in a rat breeding lab . . . My job was marking the baby rats. These were rats for laboratories. Rats for experiments, and I had to mark them by punching a series of holes in their ears when they were born; with a hole puncher. Combinations of holes for identification. They'd scream when I did it; these heart-rendering screams.

The woman who ran the rat place used to say that rats had no pain receptors in their ears. She said they screamed because they were startled.

But she loved some of the rats because they were her favorites. She'd play with them sometimes. She'd hold one of them close up under her chin and she'd be kissing it and petting and stroking it until it nuzzled into her neck with a squeak. Until the rat gave up being a rat. And then she'd just fling it against the wall

(*Horror slams her washcloth down on the table with a slap.*)

And it would leave this bloody splat and then she'd yell: CLEAN IT! CLEAN IT! CLEAN IT!

(*Horror stares at June.*)

Little rat, I do not want to clean your juice off the wall.

THE KENTUCKY CYCLE:
THE COURTSHIP OF MORNING STAR 1776
Robert Schenkkan

The Kentucky Cycle is a series of nine riveting, short plays tracing the lives of the Rowen, Talbert and Biggs families in rural Appalachian Kentucky from 1775 to 1975.

The Courtship of Morning Star 1776. Michael Rowen, 35, has kidnapped Morning Star, a young Indian girl, 16, whose tribe was wiped out by smallpox. She fights him, violently until he cuts a tendon in her leg to cripple her enough so she can't run away.

Star, in labor with Michael's child, describes her feelings for the child and its father.

♦   ♦   ♦

MORNING STAR: Everywhere is death. And I am the Noon-Day Sun who dreamed once that she was a woman named Morning Star.
(*The Double screams.*)
Where are my sisters?! Who will build my birthing hut? Where is my mother? Who will guide me through my time? Where are you, Grandmother?! Why have you turned your face from your people?! THIS CHILD WILL KILL ME!
(*The Double screams.*)
How I hated you, little one. When my blood stopped and my belly grew, how I hated you! You were a part of *him*, my enemy, only now he was inside me. No longer could I shut him out, for there you were, always! How I hated you!
(*The Double screams.*)
But when I felt you move, child, when you whispered to me that you were *mine* – aaahhh, how then I laughed at my fears! *Mine!* You are *my* blood, and *my* flesh! We are *one* breath, and *one* heartbeat, and *one* thought, and that is DEATH TO HIM!
(*The Double screams.*)
Hurry, child – how I long to hold you!

(*The Double screams.*)
Hurry, child – my breasts ache for your touch!
(*The Double screams.*)
Hurry, child, and grow strong!

THE KENTUCKY CYCLE:
A FIRE IN THE HOLE 1920
Robert Schenkkan

The Kentucky Cycle is a series of nine riveting, short plays tracing the lives of the Rowen, Talbert and Biggs families in rural Appalachian Kentucky from 1775 to 1975.

A Fire in the Hole 1920. The Rowen's land has by now been decimated by mining and conditions for the miners are horrendous and unsafe. When someone comes to organize a union, Mary Ann's husband, Tommy, fearfully betrays the union backers and their leader is executed.

Mary Ann realizes that her marriage to Tommy, whom she never loved, has been a sham. Here, she defiantly takes back her name and renounces her marriage to the man she no longer trusts.

◆　◆　◆

MARY ANN: I 'member when you was courtin' me, how mean my folks was to you and how you just stood there and took it 'cause you loved me, and even my daddy had to admit, "That Tommy Jackson, he ain't no quitter." And I thought, no he ain't. When they tore my stars down, I'da give up right then, but you wouldn't let me. I dint love you, but I thought, "They can tear these mountains apart, but Tommy Jackson won't quit on me."

I know you loved our boys, and I loved you for that. I put up with the drinkin' and you hittin' me 'cause I knew you grieved in your heart like I did and I reckon I dint think I deserved any better. You wasn't never kind, Tommy, and you weren't never wise, but I never thought you was a quitter.

And then you quit on me.

My name is Rowen. Mary Anne Rowen. I got one son, Joshua Rowen, and this man is a stranger to me.

THE KENTUCKY CYCLE:
A FIRE IN THE HOLE 1920
Robert Schenkkan

The Kentucky Cycle is a series of nine riveting, short plays tracing the lives of the Rowen, Talbert and Biggs families in rural Appalachian Kentucky from 1775 to 1975.

A Fire in the Hole 1920. The Rowen's land has by now been decimated by mining and conditions for the miners are horrendous and unsafe. When someone comes to organize a union, Mary Ann's husband, Tommy, fearfully betrays the union backers and their leader is executed.

After their leader's murder, the men are disheartened and decide to give up fighting for the union. Mary Ann and the other women are left alone, feeling helpless and defeated. Here, Mary Ann showing enormous courage and resolve, rallies the women to stand up for what they believe.

♦   ♦   ♦

MARY ANN: What's hard – dyin'?! I'll tell you what's hard: waitin' for that knock on the door and some long face from the Company sayin' they're sorry, ma'am, but there's been an accident – that's hard. Watchin' your son go down into the dark mine in the mornin' and not knowin' whether you'll ever see him again – that's hard. Buryin' a baby you just . . . I buried four children in this ground, you hear me, four babies, and I didn't have no choice about it. But I got a choice now, and I ain't buryin' another one! They can bring in a hundred goddamn armies and it cain't be nothin' worse than what we've known. It won't never stop unless we say it stops, and I say it stops now. Right now. Right here. Stand up!

THE KENTUCKY CYCLE:
TIES THAT BIND 1819
Robert Schenkkan

The Kentucky Cycle is a series of nine riveting, short plays tracing the lives of the Rowen, Talbert and Biggs families in rural Appalachian Kentucky from 1775 to 1975.

Ties That Bind 1819. Patrick Rowen, the son of Michael and Star, has gone bankrupt and is forced to sell all of the land to his sworn enemy, Jeremiah Talbert. He is then placed in the humiliating position of having to sharecrop what used to be his family's land.

Here, Patrick, who does not yet know Jeremiah's identity, begs not to be thrown off his land.

♦   ♦   ♦

PATRICK: I'm sure sorry to hear about your trouble. My . . . my pa . . . he's dead, and my wife, Becca, she died birthin' my youngest, Zachariah. So I know what . . . it's like . . . we got somethin' . . . we share somethin' here.

This here . . . this land . . . it's all I ever knowed. All I ever wanted. I know . . . know every foot of this place. I bet if you was to blind me and take me somewheres on it, any wheres, I could tell you where we was just by the smell and the taste of the dirt. I could do that. I did a wrong thing, here. I see that. And the law don't smile on no poor man when he do wrong. But my boys . . . they didn't do nothin'. You gonna toss me off'n this land, well, you gotta right to do that, but I'm askin' you to think of your own family, think of your pa and that sister of yours and let my boys stay on. I'm beggin' you. . . .

THE KENTUCKY CYCLE:
TIES THAT BIND 1819
Robert Schenkkan

The Kentucky Cycle is a series of nine riveting, short plays tracing the lives of the Rowen, Talbert and Biggs families in rural Appalachian Kentucky from 1775 to 1975.

Ties That Bind 1819. Patrick Rowen, the son of Michael and Star, has gone bankrupt and is forced to sell all of the land to his sworn enemy, Jeremiah Talbert. He is then placed in the humiliating position of having to sharecrop what used to be his family's land.

Jeremiah reveals who he is to Patrick and gloats over his revenge on the Rowens.

♦ ♦ ♦

JEREMIAH: I'm Jeremiah Talbert.

[**PATRICK:** Talbert.]

JEREMIAH: Star come get me the night you run her off. The night you killed my pa and took my sister, Rebecca. For the longest time, I was gonna kill you. But somehow that didn't seem enough – just killin' you. So I decided to let you live, but take away everythin in your life that meant anything to you, just like you done to me. And now I own you, Rowen – own all of you Rowens. (*Beat.*) You know, I never thought I'd hear myself say this, but I hope you live a long time, Patrick. I hope you live a long, long time. (*Beat.*) Two weeks from today, I spect to see all you Rowens over at what used to be the Talbert homestead. Your daddy knows the way, boys. You're gonna build your uncle Talbert a new house. With a *big* porch. And ever morning I get up I'm gonna sit on my big porch and drink a big cup of coffee and watch you Rowens workin' my land. (*Beat.*) I'm done, Judge. Court's adjourned.

THE KENTUCKY CYCLE:
THE WAR ON POVERTY 1975
Robert Schenkkan

The Kentucky Cycle is a series of nine riveting, short plays tracing the lives of the Rowen, Talbert and Biggs families in rural Appalachian Kentucky from 1775 to 1975.

The War on Poverty 1975. Joshua, Mary Ann's son, now 65, has undergone the loss of his son, Scotty, in a mining accident that was partly his fault.

Here, Joshua recounts a dream where he sees his son and his parents, who are trying to tell him something vitally important.

♦　♦　♦

JOSHUA: I keep havin' this dream.
(*Beat.*)
In my dream, I'm crossin' some kind of desert. It's all slate and ashes and dust. I hear Scotty callin' to me and I run after his voice till I come to this river. Somehow I know it's the Shillin', but it ain't nothin' like that pathetic sewer you see out there today. This is deep and wide and fulla fast-movin' muddy water. Scotty's on the other side; I can't get to 'im. And then I notice he's not alone. He's standin' there with my daddy. I haven't thought about Tommy in years, but there he is – got his minin' clothes on, coal dust on his face. I don't realize till I see'im how much I miss'im. And Momma's standin' right next to 'em, got her arm around him. And then behind them is this whole buncha people I don't know and they're all talkin' to me, yellin' somethin', but I can't hear it – the river's too loud and the wind is blowin' the dust like crazy. I know if I could just hear what they were sayin' I'd know what I was supposed to do. I'm supposed to do somethin', see, but I can't hear it, I can't hear Scotty.
(*Beat.*)
And then I wake up.

THE KENTUCKY CYCLE:
THE WAR ON POVERTY 1975
Robert Schenkkan

The Kentucky Cycle is a series of nine riveting, short plays tracing the lives of the Rowen, Talbert and Biggs families in rural Appalachian Kentucky from 1775 to 1975.

The War on Poverty 1975. Joshua, Mary Ann's son, now 65, has undergone the loss of his son, Scotty, in a mining accident that was partly his fault.

Joshua's friends are pressuring him to sell off his share of the land for strip mining, which would mean the ultimate rape of the land. In a turmoil, Joshua vividly remembers his mother, the courageous Mary Ann, and the other miners who still believed in something and were not afraid to fight for it. He comes to believe that this is the message from the dream and that, at last, he too must take a good stand.

♦   ♦   ♦

JOSHUA: [But it wasn't always like that.]
I remember that first year after the strike – you remember this big meetin' we had in Morgan? I 'member my mama and your daddy, sittin' up on this platform made outta wagons, talkin' to this huge crowd come from all over the Cumberland – men 'n' women 'n' children. I have never seen so many people before, and the mountains behind 'em seem to go on forever. And you and me they made us stand in the back 'cause we could never sit still on them platforms. You remember?
[**FRANKLIN:** Yeah, I guess.]
JOSHUA: We couldn't have been, what. . . .?
[**FRANKLIN:** I don't know.]
JOSHUA: Twelve or thirteen? And we couldn't see over the people's heads, remember? So we climbed up on top of this store. And the roof was hot, so you found us somethin' to sit on –
[**FRANKLIN:** A flour sack or somethin'.]
JOSHUA: That's right. An old flour sack. And we sat there together on this little burlap island, lookin' out over this sea of

people like the mountains in bloom in that spring my momma usta tell me about in her dreams, and they were all holdin' hands and swayin' back and forth and it was *all one thing* – all of us and them mountains – and I remember thinkin', there ain't nothin' we can't do! NOTHIN!

LIFE AFTER TIME
Paul Linke

An Actor, Paul Linke, talks about the incredible pain and difficulties he faced after the death of his wife from breast cancer. Left with three children, he must cope with their loss and come to terms with his own emotions.

Here, Paul describes his first sexual encounter after his wife's death.

♦   ♦   ♦

PAUL: I sat on the edge of the waterbed as Beth came into the room. She took off her top. I looked up at her and thought she was so beautiful. I couldn't believe that life was moving on. I was going to make love to this woman. Incredible. The next thing I knew, we were naked on the waterbed. I held her and touched her all over. I started exploring her breasts and instinctively started to check her for lumps. Well, my wife had died of breast cancer, right? I caught myself wondering whether she was aware of what I was doing. I began asking myself these esoteric questions. How long do you go out with a woman before you ask her to have a mammogram? Do you go steady and then ask her to get a pap smear? Was I going to spend my honeymoon at the Mayo Clinic? I pulled back, "I can't do this. I don't know you well enough, Beth. I can't have sex with you. We don't have a relationship. I don't know what it means."

THE MIND WITH THE DIRTY MAN
Jules Tasca

Wayne Stone and his wife, Alma, are upstanding members of the Buckram Movie Review Board, doing their best to keep dirty movies out of Buckram. The only problem is that their son and his wife make x-rated movies. Also, Wayne and Alma both feel stifled and bored with their routine love life. When Alma places a personal ad for the "company of sexy mature male," the ad is answered by her own husband.

Here Alma tries to explain to her son why she felt compelled to place the personals ad.

♦   ♦   ♦

ALMA: Please forget about this ad. It's just a sign of old age, that's all. You get scared that it's all over, so you get daring. You get desperate for something to tell you, "Alma, you're not that far gone. There're a lot of men who'd love to be romantic with you. You just don't have the opportunity." Then you get a little crêpey around the neck and scared stiff that you're just your husband's wash woman, so you do something stupid like that ad. I've been trying to get him to retire and give us both more of a life. But that's as far as I can go. I thought you'd understand. Do you know since you came home here with that fetish film, he takes three scalding hot baths a day? If he finds out about this *Beard and Sandal* add, he'll go west and throw himself into Old Faithful.

THE MIND WITH THE DIRTY MAN
Jules Tasca

Wayne Stone and his wife, Alma, are upstanding members of the Buckram Movie Review Board, doing their best to keep dirty movies out of Buckram. The only problem is that their son and his wife make x-rated movies. Also, Wayne and Alma both feel stifled and bored with their routine love life. When Alma places a personal ad for the "company of sexy mature male," the ad is answered by her own husband.

Wayne, having imbibed too much wine, drunkenly confesses his past indiscretions to his wife.

♦ ♦ ♦

WAYNE: Hypocrisy! I can say it. A few sips of wine and I can say it. Hypocrisy. It's all out now. (*He pours a little more wine and sits on the Left arm of the sofa.*) Wayne Stone. President of his company. Chairman of the Citizen's Review Board. Leader in the Knights of Columbus. Respected member of the church and part-time pig! (*Wayne raises his glass to toast and Alma joins in.*) When I go to Baltimore once a month for the Board of Directors meeting, Alma, I stand on the street corner and wink at girls. Or I hang around the Friendship Airport bar and try to pick up stewardesses. Once, one of them said yes. I got scared and flew home under your brother-in-law's name to throw off the air police. Alma, I'm sorry. Hollow as it sounds. I'm sorry.

MUZEEKA
John Guare

Muzeeka was written in 1968 as an anti-war satire. Jack Argue conducts the orchestra for Muzeeka, a company that creates bland "elevator music." Argue is drafted and sent to Vietnam, where he finds that he enjoys fighting and killing more than his life with his wife and job back home.

Here, Jack tells his wife that he deeply admires the ancient and mysterious peoples, the Etruscans, more than anyone he can think of.

♦   ♦   ♦

ARGUE: If I could've been born anybody – my pick of a Kennedy or a Frank Sinatra or a Henry Ford or the King of Greece – out of that whole hat of births, I still would've picked to be an Etruscan. Nobody knows where they came from. The archaeologists guess maybe they were one of the first tribes of Rome about a million years ago when Romulus and Remus were posing for that Roman statue – that baby picture – of them suckling life from a wolf. Well, Romulus and old Uncle Remus must've hoarded all that wolf milk to themselves because the Etruscans vanished without a trace, like a high, curved wave that breaks on the sand and retreats right back into the sea. Vanished. Poof. Splash.
And the only footprints the Etruscans left behind were these jugs. These jugs and pots and bottles and urns covered with pictures. Line drawings much like Picasso's. The whole world can sue me for libel but I accuse Pablo Picasso of stealing all his line drawings from the Etruscans. J'accuse! J'accuse Pablo Picasso! Pots and jugs covered with people dancing. ALL dancing. Warriors dancing. Men dancing. Women dancing. Servants dancing. Prostitutes dancing. Old men with bottles of wine and they're *dancing*. A whole civilization dancing. Every part of them *dancing*. Not just their feet, but their hands and heads and beards and peckers and bosoms and shoulders and noses and toes all dancing. And these smiles – these lovely, loony smiles – that should make them look like a race of

Alfred E. Neumans except only genius could know the joy that's painted on those pots and bottles and urns. All painted in earth colors: blacks and browns and tans and white. A whole civilization danced up out of the earth. Danced up out of the ground all over the ground and vanished. Maybe they just danced right into the pots and what we see being held prisoner in museums is not line drawings of Etruscans, but the Etruscans themselves, dancing right inside the pots. If I could've been born anybody in the world ever – my pick of a Kennedy or Sinatra or Henry Ford or the King of Greece – I still would've picked out of that whole hat of births, picked Etruscan.

MUZEEKA
John Guare

Muzeeeka was written in 1968 as an anti-war satire. Jack Argue conducts the orchestra for Muzeeka, a company that creates bland "elevator music." Argue is drafted and sent to Vietnam, where he finds that he enjoys fighting and killing more than his life with his wife and job back home.

Jack reveals a secret plan he has formulated for Muzeeka once he has accepted a job there.

♦ ♦ ♦

ARGUE: I'll start first with the violins. The Old Give 'Em What They Want. I'll wait with my tongue in my cheek here like a private smirking soul kiss and when I'm piped into every elevator, every office, every escalator, every toilet, every home, airplane, bus, truck, and car in this country, I'll strike. (*The stagehands fade away. Argue turns full to us.*)
Do you know about the cortical overlay that covers fifty percent of the human brain, deadening all our instincts so we have to be given lessons in every facet of living – except dying, of course. The human and the dolphin are the only animals that have this clay pot on the brain. How the dolphins manage to survive, I can't figure out. But they'll have to take care of themselves. I'm involved with the humans.
I'll wait 'til all humans are inured to the ever-present, inescapable background ocean blandness of my music, 'til everyone knows down deep I'll always be there, stroking that cortical overlay 'til it's as hard and brittle as the clay of an Etruscan pot and then, on a sudden day that is not especially Spring, not especially Summer, a day when the most exciting thing around is the new issue of the *Reader's Digest*, and you read with interest an ad that says Campbell just invented a new flavor soup, I'll *strike*. That kind of a day. I'll pipe in my own secret music that I keep hidden here under my cortical overlay and I'll free all the Etruscans in all our brains. Not rock and roll. No, more than that. A blend of Rock and Mozart and

Wagnerian Lieberstods and Gregorian chants. Eskimo folk songs. African. Greek. Hindu. All bound together by drums that will fascistically force its *way* through the over*lay* and the country will remember its Etruscan forebearers and begin dancing. (*The stagehands begin dancing, writhing, in the dark background. Their heavy breathing mounts in passion.*)

I'll sit in my office turning the level of volume louder and louder and watch the fires in the distance as men throw in their attaché cases, their Buicks, their split level homes and mortgages and commuter tickets and railroad trains and husbands and wives and children and bosses and enemies and friends.

On planes, pilots will race to the sea and passengers will slug the smiles off stewardesses and stewardesses will pour hot coffee on all the regular passengers.

Bald people – hairless men, hairless ladies – will whip off their wigs and eyebrows and grease their skulls and bodies with black car grease so the moon will reflect on them when they dance.

Everybody will feel sexy all the time and nobody will mind what anybody does to anybody else and twins in wombs will dance so that girl babies will be born with babies within them and those babies will have babies within them and within them and within and within.

Busses gallop down Fifth Avenue crammed with naked people beeping the horn, riding on the sidewalk, looting all the stores, making love in all the churches, knocking noses off plaster saints and never getting out of the bus.

Busses gallop down Fifth Avenue crammed with naked people eating pictures of Chinese food off the posters in the subway and the train pulls in and all of the naked people push the train off the tracks and leap onto the third rail to see what electricity tastes like.

They race up to Harlem where naked people have flooded the streets with fat and are chicken-frying Puerto Ricans who cha cha cha and everybody's skin blisters and crackles in cha cha time. The Negroes skewer white people onto maracas and we all dance and devour each other and *belch* and nobody dies because we've forgotten to and our rib cages become bars of music and our eyes and ears behind the rib cages are notes of music and our spines are staff notes holding us up high and everyone's body is a dance floor and the dancing sets our planet loose and we'll tumble around in galaxies *until*, in exhaustion, the world will settle back into place and rest and rest and we shall have the beautiful peace of exhaustion. (*The stagehands exit*.)

For that is all peace is – isn't it – exhaustion? The peace of sadness. After copulation all men are sad? And the peace will be sad and slow of breath and even a vague disgust . . .

But there will be exhaustion and, yes, a contentment and, yes, there shall be peace . . .

MY CRUMMY JOB
John Steppling

My Crummy Job is the story of three discontented and disconnected people who come together and talk during their breaks from their low paying, dead-end jobs. Ike, a shoe salesman who has knocked around the country in various low-end sales jobs, enjoys confiding in Paige, a young, divorced waitress.

Paige has become involved with Junior, an angry man who works with Ike. Here, referring to her ex-husband, Deak, Paige talks about driving past the homes of the wealthy in Brentwood.

◆   ◆   ◆

PAIGE: Deak used to say, "Bite the scorpion," you know – if you're gonna get down – you "bite the scorpion" – you don't just talk – talk is cheap. Conversation, there is nothing cheaper than conversation.
(*Pause. Paige looks at him , then turns away.*)
I just want to pay the rent. Simple things. I'd like to just know the rent will be there. (*Pause.*) If you work, that things will get better. That's all, that's all. (*Pause.*) You ever drive through Beverly Hills, Brentwood, and wonder where did all these people get money – how did they all get so much money? There's a *lot* of nice houses we're talking about. A lot.

PH*REAKS
Doris Baizley and Victoria Ann-Lewis

In *PH*Reaks*, as in life, people with disabilities not only have to cope with the difficulties presented by their handicaps, but must deal with the greater obstacles placed by a society rife with ignorance, fear and insensitivity.

Father John, representing religious zealots, perpetuates the discrimination experienced by the disabled. Here, he warns all who will listen that the devil lives in the crippled and deformed.

◆ ◆ ◆

FATHER JOHN: Beware, careless souls. I saw with mine own eyes the marks of their tongs upon his mangled tongue. The devil's slaves had silenced the beast so he would not reveal their Master's secrets. These are the same devils that roar in the deaf man's ears so he cannot hear the words of Light. These are the same darknesses that curl inside the hunchback's burden. Have you not smelled the sulfur as these monsters pass?
(*Slides: Old woodcuts of ancient gods, acts of bestiality.*)
Beware: The devil grew bold in the old days. He came as a swan or a bull. He called himself Zeus or Pan and he made men hungry for the dark. "Roman women often bare their buttocks to donkeys, inducing the beasts to mount them" Juvenal the Pagan Historian tells us.
(*Slides: Satyrs, Fauns, and Devils.*)
Beware careless souls: satyrs, fauns, the devil still comes to tempt. Some weak souls fall. Pretending to sleep, they invite Lucifer himself into their beds and find him beautiful. But when the woman sees the repulsive issue of that union, when the monster claws out between her legs, she is grateful for the kindness that ties her filthy body to the stake and burns it clean.
(*Slides: Giants, Dwarves, Gnomes, Mermaids, and Hunchbacks, including Danny De Vito as the penguin in Batman.*)
Wise men of old times have condemned these offspring of the

devil. "Deformed and infirm children should be hidden away in a secret place" Plato tells us. Aristotle advises they should not be fed.

PH*REAKS
Doris Baizley and Victoria Ann-Lewis

In *PH*Reaks*, as in life, people with disabilities not only have to cope with the difficulties presented by their handicaps, but must deal with the greater obstacles placed by a society rife with ignorance, fear and insensitivity.

Angie, a dwarf, angrily responds when a Doctor asks her why she displays herself in a side-show. Why shouldn't they *pay* to look at her when she is stared and gawked at all the time anyway?

♦   ♦   ♦

ANGIE: Listen, smart boy, it's easy – we're always on display. You think that if I walked down the street of your stinking little nowhere town people wouldn't stare at me? Damn right they would, and tell their neighbors and friends and talk about me over dinners and picnics and PTA meetings. Well, if they want to do that, they're going to have to pay me for that privilege. You want to stare at me, fine, it's 25 cents, cash on the barrel. You want a picture, that's another quarter. My life story? Pay me. You think I'm being exploited? You pay to go to a baseball game, don't you? What's the difference if you watch some big oaf hitting a ball with a stick or me pretending to be a princess?

THE SHADOW BOX
Michael Cristofer

The Shadow Box is the story of three terminally ill people staying in hospice cottages and how each of them deals with their illness and their loved ones.

Joe is visited by his wife, Maggie, who can't accept his illness, and his teenage son. Here, he reveals the nightmare he has every night.

♦ ♦ ♦

JOE: I get dreams now. Every night. I get dreams so big. I never used to dream. But now, every night, so big. Every person I ever knew in my life coming through my room, talking and talking and sometimes singing and dancing. Jumping all around my bed. And I get up to go with them, but I can't. The sheets are too heavy and I can't move to save my life. And they keep talking and calling my name, whispering so loud it hurts my ears . . . 'Joe' and 'Joe' and laughing and singing and I know every one of them and they pull at my arms and my legs and I still can't move. And I'm laughing and singing, too, inside, where you can't hear it. And it hurts so bad, but I can't feel it. And I yell back at them, every person I ever knew, and they don't hear me, either, and then the room gets brighter and brighter. So bright I can't see anything anymore. Nobody. Not even me. Its all gone. All white. All gone.

THE SHADOW BOX
Michael Cristofer

The Shadow Box is the story of three terminally ill people staying in hospice cottages and how each of them deals with their illness and their loved ones.

Brian, a gay man, is being cared for by his lover, Mark. Brian angrily responds to the fuss his wife and lover are making over a champagne stain on Mark's jacket.

♦   ♦   ♦

BRIAN: (*Grabbing the jacket and throwing it down.*) My God, it's only a jacket. Two sleeves, a collar, a piece of cloth. It was probably made by a machine in East Podunk. Why are we wasting this time?

[**MARK:** Brian, take it easy . . .]

BRIAN: [No! Not easy. Not easy at all!] At this very moment, twelve million stars are pumping light in and out of a three hundred and sixty degree notion of a limited universe. Not easy. At this very moment, a dozen Long Island oysters are stranded in some laboratory in Chicago, opening and closing to the rhythm of the tide – over a thousand miles away. Not easy. At this very moment, the sun is probably hurtling out of control, defying ninety percent of all organized religion – plummeting toward a massive world collision that was predicted simultaneously by three equally archaic cultures who had barely invented the wheel. At this very moment, some simple peasant in Mexico is planting seeds in his veins with the blind hope that flowers will bloom on his body before the frost kills him! And here we stand, the combined energy of our three magnificent minds focused irrevocably on a jacket. (*He puts the jacket on sofa to dry.*) My God. There are more important things, I promise you.

THE SHADOW BOX
Michael Cristofer

The Shadow Box is the story of three terminally ill people staying in hospice cottages and how each of them deals with their illness and their loved ones.

Brian, a gay man, is being cared for by his lover, Mark. Here, his ex-wife, Beverly, warns Mark that Brian is using him.

◆　◆　◆

BEVERLY: Let me tell you something, as one whore to another – what you do with your ass is your business. You can drag it through every gutter from here to Morocco. You can trade it, sell it or give it away. You can run it up a flagpole, paint it blue or cut it off if you feel like it. I don't care. I'll even show you the best way to do it. That's the kind of person I am. But Brian is different. Because Brian is stupid. Because Brian is blind. Because Brian doesn't know where you come from or who you come from or why or how or even what you are coming to. Because Brian happens to need you. And if that is not enough for you, then you get yourself out of his life – fast. You take your delicate sensibilities and your fears and your disgust, if that's all you feel, and you pack it up and you get out.

THE SHADOW BOX
Michael Cristofer

The Shadow Box is the story of three terminally ill people staying in hospice cottages and how each of them deals with their illness and their loved ones. Joe is visited by his wife, Maggie.

Maggie, defiantly and still in denial, tells Joe she wants him to come home with her.

♦   ♦   ♦

MAGGIE: [No. I want you to come home.] What is this place, anyway? They make everything so nice. Why? So you forget? I can't. I can't. I want you to come home. I want you to stay out four nights a week bowling, and then come home so I can yell and not talk to you, you son of a bitch. I want to fight so you'll take me to a movie and by the time I get you to take me I'm so upset I can't enjoy the picture. I want to get up too early, too goddamn early, and I'll let you know about it, too, because I have to make you breakfast, because you never, never once eat it, because you make me get up too early just to keep you company and talk to you, and it's cold, and my back aches, and I got nothing to say to you and we never talk and it's six-thirty in the morning, *every* morning, even Sunday morning and it's all right . . . it's all right . . . it's all right because I *want* to be there because you need me to be there because I want *you* to be there because I want you to come home.

STALIN'S DAUGHTER
August Baker

Stalin's Daughter, set in 1969, is three separate stories linked by the Vietnam War and its effect on the real and fictional people in the play. This play explores the repercussions of war on the lives of people who are touched by it directly and indirectly. Sharon Tate is interviewed just *after* her brutal murder by the Manson gang.

After describing the evening leading up to the murders, Sharon describes the murders themselves.

♦   ♦   ♦

SHARON: Then a woman . . . came into my room . . .
(*Video cuts to a black cat licking its paws.*)
Carrying a knife. (*Slight pause.*) She told us to go into the living room . . . and when we got there Abby and Voytek were sitting on the couch. Bound. Scared. (*Slight pause.*) She pushed us down beside them, and another woman and man came in from the kitchen and started circling round us. (*Beat.*) Then the man waved a gun and told us to lie on the floor, on our stomachs, but Jay started arguing with him – saying I couldn't do that – because of the baby. (*Two beats.*) So he shot him. Dead. Like he was nothing.
(*Slight pause.*)
[**SPOOK:** And then . . . Sharon?]
SHARON: Then the man handed one of the women a rope, and she wrapped it around our necks and threw one end over a beam in the ceiling so that we had to stand on our toes to keep from choking. And when Abby asked what was going to happen, the man said, 'You're all going to die.'
(*She begins to hyperventilate.*)
[**SPOOK:** Sharon . . .]
SHARON: (*Pressured.*) We screamed. Just kept screaming, while the woman with the knife came closer and closer to Voytek. (*Beat.*) Then somehow he broke free, but she started stabbing him, over and over again, until he ran out the front door – bleeding, yelling for help – the man chasing after him. (*Beat.*)

53

Then Abby broke free too and started fighting with the other woman. And everybody was fighting except me, because I couldn't get loose. I just couldn't get loose, so all I could do was watch and scream knowing we were all going to die. (*Beat*.) And that I would be the last. The witness.

STALIN'S DAUGHTER
August Baker

Stalin's Daughter, set in 1969, is three separate stories linked by the Vietnam War and its effect on the real and fictional people in the play. This play explores the repercussions of war on the lives of people who are touched by it directly and indirectly.

Richard Nixon is being interviewed by Dr. Rita Gains, a psychiatrist. Here, Nixon describes a botched bombing attempt in Vietnam.

♦ ♦ ♦

NIXON: It began in March. March 15th. (*Beat.*) I can still remember the day. (*Slight pause.*) Before that we'd had the intelligence . . . *thought* the thing could be done. But it wasn't until March that we got the green light from the brass. (*Slight pause.*) I was told that the brains – the headquarters – would be there. That we could just go in and destroy all thought. All operations. That it would be quick. Efficient. We could just go in and decapitate them with one good strike. (*Beat.*) And so based on that I said, 'Let's do it. Let's just go in there and decapitate them.'
(*He automatically starts to pour a drink, then catches himself.*)
(*Slow rising anger.*) So we did go in . . . with air strikes. (*Beat.*) But the head wasn't even there. The intelligence just turned out to be shit. (*Beat.*) And to make matters worse, we didn't even kill what was there. (*Beat.*) Those were the orders. *Kill everything.* (*Beat.*) But they didn't. They failed. The bombers failed and that cost us lives on the ground. (*Beat.*) One. Two. Maybe three made it back, but the rest of the unit was just butchered. (*Beat.*) So we ordered in a second squad, but they wouldn't budge. They just said, 'Fuck you. We won't go.' (*Beat.*) This was passed on to me, you see. What they said. (*Beat.*) 'Fuck *you,*' to the President!

STALIN'S DAUGHTER
August Baker

Stalin's Daughter, set in 1969, is three separate stories linked by the Vietnam War and its effect on the real and fictional people in the play. This play explores the repercussions of war on the lives of people who are touched by it directly and indirectly.

Megan, a young woman who lives in Princeton, New Jersey, reveals to her parents an earlier incident between her brother, who is missing in action in Vietnam, and their celebrity neighbor, Stalin's daughter.

♦ ♦ ♦

MEGAN: About two years ago – just after our neighbor moved here – Ronny and I were walking home from school. (*Beat.*) And as we pass her house, she pulls up in a limousine – with some security men – wearing sunglasses. (*Slight pause.*) The chauffeur opens her door, she starts to climb out, then sees *us.* (*Beat.*) And just stops and sits there. (*Beat.*) Like she's frozen. (*Slight pause.*) One of the men comes over and touches her arm, but she brushes him off, walks over, sort of looks right through us and says: 'I left behind my daughter and son.' (*Beat.*) 'But I've asked to be forgiven.' (*Beat.*) 'Understand I can no longer be an enemy to myself.' (*Pause.*) I'm shaking all over. (*Beat.*) And Ronny's not only shaking. There are tears in his eyes. (*Two beats.*) But for some reason he leans over . . . and kisses her . . . on the cheek. (*Pause.*) One of the men runs over and grabs Ronny, but she grabs the man and hollers, 'Let go! The boy is a gift!' (*Two beats.*) Then turns and walks into her house.

STANDUP TRAGEDY
Bill Cain

This play, set in a Catholic school for Hispanic boys in lower East-side Manhattan, relates a teacher's experience with the tragedy of inner-city violence, death and despair.

Father Ed Larkin, a Jesuit priest and principal of the school, reveals that he is disillusioned with a God who proves His love by allowing His Son to die.

♦　　♦　　♦

LARKIN: The kids in this school . . . the kids in this school are the only children I will ever have. For a few years, they're mine. And I don't like the way God treats them. God. The creator of the Pleides . . . the Wonderful . . . the Counselor . . . the Mighty God . . . the Everlasting Father . . . Father? The God, who – in the goodness of his heart – saved Moses' children . . . by killing Pharaoh's children. The God who saved us all . . . by actually killing his only son. If a parent in the neighborhood behaved like that, I'd call a cop. What cop do I call? (*A loud cry in an empty church*:) *I need a better God.* (*After brief pause*:) Technically that's blasphemy . . . which is the most serious of sins . . . and the only one I commit more than once a day. He doesn't like it, he can hit me with a thunderbolt. He might even be doing me a favor because I'm pretty fucking sick of poverty, chastity and obedience at this stage of the game. (*Kneeling*:) Say the prayers for the dead for our children.

STANDUP TRAGEDY
Bill Cain

This play, set in a Catholic school for Hispanic boys in lower East-side Manhattan, relates a teacher's experience with the tragedy of inner-city violence, death and despair.

Tom Griffin, an increasingly cynical teacher, describes his frustration when trying to find a battered women's shelter for the mother of one of his students.

◆　◆　◆

GRIFFIN: (*Laughing/crying.*) So Lee's mother wouldn't do anything about the notice to evict and – with Ty and Lee gone – sure as hell she'd end up in the streets so I thought, Shit, I've got to get this lady some housing. So I found her this home for battered women, but when we get there, they say to me there's no room in the inn, and I say, Wait a minute, you told me . . . No, that was two weeks ago, they say. I say, So what? She's here now. And they say they couldn't hold a place for her. There are other homeless people, you know. So I say – So what? Throw them out. They've been homeless before. They're used to it.

[**LARKIN:** (*Dressed in formal clerical attire.*) Counterproductive.]

GRIFFIN: (*Through fierce, bitter laughter.*) And it gets crazier and crazier every place we go. The last place we went, they told me she was beaten by *the wrong person*. I said what the fuck do you mean? I know. Counterproductive. And they say, we only accept women who've been beaten by their husbands. We don't believe it's serious if she's beaten by a son. And I say, What are you talking about? Her husbands are old and slow; the kid is in his prime and full of drugs and they say, Sorry, we have our rules and I say, No, wait, I'm her husband. I beat her all the time. I'll beat her here and now if you'll give her a room.

STRUCK DUMB
Jean-Claude van Itallie and Joseph Chaikin

Struck Dumb is a one-character play about a man with aphasia; that is, his speech and comprehension are "out of phase" due to a stroke. The lines are not memorized but read, as would be necessary for an aphasic actor.

Adnan, a middle-aged aphasic, explains his daily routine since his stroke.

◆ ◆ ◆

ADNAN: My name is Adnan.
I was born in Beirut, in Lebanon,
In a big house.
Beirut, it's an ancient city.
Lebanon, my country,
Five thousand years ago,
It was called Phoenicia.
Now I am living in Venice, California.
I have a bedroom, and a kitchen.
It's morning: I have coffee, and then breakfast:
Toast or something.
I'm eating something – it's a muffin.
It's "taste." I'm amazed –
Shock.
(*Adnan listens.*)
Tremor, quake – it's shaking again.
Earth groaning again.
(*Adnan listens, then returns to normal.*)
This room has only three or four things.
Simple, it's better, it's best.
This is my desk. It's wood.
The desk exists longer than I am human,
Longer than my father, longer than my grandfather.
It's from the Shakers.
These are my tapes.
Music, it's pulse and rhythm and melody.
I see music.

My greatest pleasure, it's music, hearing God.
Then, second, it's colors.
I have pleasure also from shapes – like shells, from the sea.
Music, it might be shapes.
Thinking about shapes, shells.
Bodies –
Like air, like clouds . . .
For example spiders – many legs, many arms.
Spiders to galaxy, spinning . . . spiral.
Shapes. . .
(*Adnan gestures a spiral shape.*)
This is my clock. It's new.
Time – oh, yes – it's important to me now,
It's order.
Without clock, one second or one year – no different.
But when I leave my house,
When I go to the ocean,
When I'm looking at the sea,
I do not want a clock at all.

STRUCK DUMB
Jean-Claude van Itallie and Joseph Chaikin

Struck Dumb is a one-character play about a man with aphasia; that is, his speech and comprehension are "out of phase" due to a stroke. The lines are not memorized but read, as would be necessary for an aphasic actor.

Adnan talks about a little dog he likes and man's relationship with animals.

◆　　◆　　◆

ADNAN: Every day, on the street,
I meet a dog.
I'm looking into her eyes.
She's looking at me.
She's cute: a thousand curlies, her hair.
It's golden and it's brown,
Like cashew, the nut.
She's not my dog really, but almost.
Her name is Cashew.
Not really, but I love the name "Cashew."
Cashew's happy to see me.
(*Adnan is greeting the dog.*)
Hello. Hi, Cashew, hi.
She's jumping, she's happy.
But animals not thinking.
Cashew, she's smart.
And she's graceful
Like a ballet dancer,
But she's not thinking at all.
Animals do not drink tea, or coffee, like humans.
Animals are different.
Thinking, it's humans' . . .
Humans' what?
What is thinking?
No answer.
What is endless . . . endless . . . endless?

Eternity – what is it?
No answer.
When body is finished,
What happens to soul?
No answer.
Is something continuing?
What is it?
No answer.
Does Cashew have a soul also?
No answer.
Before, I didn't know I had a soul.
Now that I know, what to do?
What to do with my soul?
I am like: "Man struck dumb after writing letter to God."
Writing: "Dear God, I'm tired of my life.
Please send me something new."
So God strikes him dumb.
It's dangerous, writing a letter to God.
You sometimes get what you want.

TAPDANCER
Conrad Bishop and Elizabeth Fuller

Described as a "realist fantasy," *Tapdancer* relates the experiences of a 33-year-old investment broker named Kenneth. Kenneth, who defines himself as a very boring person and is described by others as "straight" and "square," decides to take a walk on the wild side. He begins by taking tapdancing lessons, followed by an affair with his bi-sexual sales assistant, ending with his decision to spray paint an offensive billboard which says: "America is Burgerland." But being a good citizen he leaves his name and address behind, in order to pay the appropriate fine. Instead he gets caught up in an insane and illogical court system akin to Alice's Wonderland. The upshot is that he gains notoriety and is ultimately sentenced to death.

Here, the prosecutor, whose name is Maggie Thatcher, makes her summation to the jury.

♦ ♦ ♦

PROSECUTOR: Ladies and gentlemen, this is a difficult case.
To what extent is actual evidence vital to conviction? My first answer would be "Well we're in a court of law."
But can we settle for easy answers? Don't we need fresh ideas? That, in some cases, guilt is not a requirement for conviction. Is that wrong for a free society? Or is it the very thing that makes our society free?
What is freedom? I say, and maybe I'm sentimental about this, that's ok, call me what you want, I say freedom is . . .
(*Gentle background chorus: "This Land Is Your Land."*)
A lawn in front of your house. A parking place for both your cars.
Looking down the highway, there's a McDonald's or Burger King, and nobody's going to make that choice for me. Freedom is playing the Lottery, and nobody says you don't have a chance. You have that chance. You have hope. You have all the hope in the world, a lifetime supply.
That's why we're here. You know in your gut there's something very wrong, I don't have to tell you. Is this a trivial case? You can believe that. Or you can choose not to believe

it. That's what freedom means: believe what you want to believe. So just think a minute . . .

(*Dead silence.*)

About the ozone layer.

Think about your health insurance and how long you'll keep it. Those people who can't even speak English, and they want your job; people with skin so dark you can't see if they're even there, and they want equal rights. Can you deal with equal rights? What happens to that edge that you, and your kids, you've worked so hard to deserve? That extra edge.

The Haves and the Have Nots. Are you a Have? Maybe today, what about tomorrow? To them that have, it will be given, and from them that have not, it will all be taken away. That's in the Bible, and the Bible means exactly what it says.

Listen to your heart. Isn't it time somebody did something, anything? – Isn't any action better than doing nothing? – Isn't it time for me to think about Me? – To send a signal? – To say "THIS IS A NEW DAY IN THE WORLD! INCLUDE ME IN!"

Then, my friends, you'll vote to convict. Cause it'll feel so good.

(*Applause. Cheers. Prosecutor goes berserk.*)

Stop! You idiots! You fell for that? Why are you all such an easy fuck? God, I don't believe it! Those words don't mean anything! I'm sticking it in your ear! I'm fucking your brains!

THE TRIAL OF THE CATONSVILLE NINE
Daniel Berrigan

The Trail of the Catonsville Nine is based on an actual incident in which nine Catholic priests were arrested and tried for burning draft records in Catonsville, Md., in protest to the Vietnam War.

At the play's opening, Daniel Berrigan, 49, a Jesuit Priest and chief defendant, recalls the day he was ordained and his feelings about the priesthood.

◆　◆　◆

DANIEL BERRIGAN: On a June morning, I lay before the altar in the chapel to be ordained a priest and the voice of Cardinal Cushing shook the house like a great war horse. His hands lay on my head like a stone. I remember a kind of desolation, the cold of the floor on which I stretched like a corpse, while the invocation of the saints went over me like a tide, a death. Would these bones live? I arose to my feet and went out in the sunshine and gave my blessing to those who had borne with me, who had waited for me. A most unfinished man. What would it mean to be a Catholic? Who would be my teacher? It was, finally, the world, the world we breathe in, the only stage of redemption, the men and women who toil in it, sin in it, suffer and die in it. Apart from them, as I came to know, the priesthood was a pallid, vacuumatic enclosure, a sheepfold for sheep. (*Discards the reading desk.*) Priests? Why priests kept their peace, muttered the Mass, sidestepped queasily the public horror, made Jesus mild as milk, a temple eunuch. I don't want to miss the action, but I must tell you my brother Phil and I were in jail at the same time last year – he for that little business of pouring blood on draft records and I for marching on the Pentagon. Those prison blue jeans and denim shirts! It's a clerical attire I highly recommend for a new church. As Camus said – (*Laughs.*) I love to talk to people but I've got to get to a burning. *Oremus pro fratribus in periculo.* (*Defendants begin in pantomiming the burning of draft files; Daniel Berrigan crosses L.*) Imagine nine felonious Catholics, jerky, harried as Keystone Cops, running out of a building bearing baskets heaped with trash, dumping them out, setting them alight, dancing like dervishes around the fire. The TV cameras ground it out, those four or five minutes when our past went up in flames whirling like ashes down a parking lot, then sober. As the flames died we joined hands praying, "Our Father who art in heaven." The film impounded rests in peace in FBI archives.

THE TRIAL OF THE CATONSVILLE NINE
Daniel Berrigan

The Trial of the Catonsville Nine is based on an actual incident in which nine Catholic priests were arrested and tried for burning draft records in Catonsville, Md., in protest to the Vietnam War.

Mary Moylan, a young nurse, while on the stand, describes the incident that awakened her social consciousness.

♦   ♦   ♦

MARY MOYLAN: For me, the political turning point in my life came while I was in Uganda. I was working as a nurse midwife with the White Sisters of Africa at Fort Portal up near the Mountains of the Moon. While I was in Uganda, American planes began bombing the Congo and we were very close to the Congo border. The planes came over and bombed two villages in Uganda, supposedly by accident. What were American planes, piloted by émigré Cubans, doing bombing in the Congo anyway? As far as I knew, the United Nations was the peace-keeping force in the Congo. Where the hell did the American planes come in? If you will excuse the language, Your Honor. This made me very interested in our foreign policy.

[DEFENSE: And under what circumstances did you leave Uganda?]

MARY MOYLAN: A serious conflict finally developed between myself and the Administrator of Hospitals. I said I loved Fort Portal very much and that I was seriously thinking about renewing my contract, but that there were several things I must object to. It was becoming obvious to me that the present setup of missions was largely irrelevant and not able to take part in the changes that were necessary in the African countries. I felt that the Africans should have more responsibility. Much of our role seemed to be to provide a white face in the black community.

THE WAITING ROOM
Lisa Loomer

This is a play about power – those who have it and feel entitled, and those who don't and try to find it. Set in New York City, England, and China, in the past, present, and "both at once," three women, each from a different time and place, find themselves on common ground in the waiting room of a doctor's office. They exchange small talk, each revealing the ways she has been oppressed. Forgiveness, an 18th-century Chinese woman, has had her feet cruelly bound in order to appear helpless and attractive to her husband. Victoria, an English woman from the 19th-century, is bound by both her corset and her time. She has been convinced that she must have her ovaries removed in order to cure her hysteria. Wanda, a 20th-century woman from New York, has had breast implants, lipo-suction, and facial surgery in order to beat the statistical odds and marry after the age of 35. Now her breasts have hardened and she suspects there might be more sinister complications.

Victoria confides to Wanda and Forgiveness that her husband, a physician, has convinced her that removal of her ovaries will get rid of her "hysteria" which manifests itself in biting, and an arm spasm which causes her to hit her husband. In fact, her arm flings involuntarily whenever she utters the word, "husband."

♦   ♦   ♦

VICTORIA: What am I being treated for? Oh . . . (*Yawns.*) hysteria. It's a disease of the ovaries. the ovaries control the personality, you see. I've done some reading on the matter. Though my—(*Her arm flings involuntarily.*) husband says that reading makes me worse. Romantic novels especially. (Proud.) My husband is a doctor. In fact, it was he that proscribed the rest cure. (*Smiles.*) Six weeks on one's back in a dimly lit room . . . no reading, no visitors, no . . . potty. I came out screaming, actually. But it was hardly my husband's fault. It seems—well, it seems I've had too much education and my uterus has atrophied commensurately. So we've decided to have the ovaries removed. (*Distraught.*) Well, we've tried everything else. Injections to the womb . . . water, milk, tea, a decoction of marshmallow. I've stopped reading and writing, stopped stimulating my emotions with operas and French plays. Last week the doctor placed leeches on my vulva. (*Wanda's mouth falls open*.) Some were quite adventurous and traveled all the way to the cervical cavity! The pressure from the corset's forced my uterus out through my vagina . . . (*With mounting hysteria*.) And according to my husband, my hysteria's only getting *worse!* The doctor says I've all the classic symptoms of ovarian disease: troublesomeness, eating like a ploughman, painful menstruation, a desire to learn Greek! – attempted suicide, persecution mania, and simple cussedness! Last night I sneezed continuously for twenty-seven minutes, and tried to *bite* my own husband! What can I do!? I shan't be beaten across the face and body with wet towels like an Irish woman! – I JUST WANT THE DAMN THINGS OUT!

THE WAITING ROOM
Lisa Loomer

This is a play about power – those who have it and feel entitled, and those who don't and try to find it. Set in New York City, England, and China, in the past, present, and "both at once," three women, each from a different time and place, find themselves on common ground in the waiting room of a doctor's office. They exchange small talk, each revealing the ways she has been oppressed. Forgiveness, an 18th-century Chinese woman, has had her feet cruelly bound in order to appear helpless and attractive to her husband. Victoria, a woman from 19th-century England, is bound by both her corset and her time. She has been convinced that she must have her ovaries removed in order to cure her hysteria. Wanda, a 20th-century woman from New York, has had breast implants, lipo-suction, and facial surgery in order to beat the statistical odds and marry after the age of 35. Now her breasts have hardened and she suspects there might be more sinister complications.

Wanda has been told that she has a tumor in her breast which may be malignant. She will need a biopsy as soon as possible. When she leaves the office, she goes across the street to get drunk. Downing double Jack Daniels', she describes to the bartender, and anyone within earshot, the bet she made with her mother to beat the statistic and marry by age 40, which she is now.

♦　　♦　　♦

WANDA: See I made a bet with my mother five years ago after I read this article she sent me from *Newsweek* while I was waiting to get a pap smear. The article said the odds of my getting married by forty were not quite as good as the odds of my being shot by a terrorist. I wonder how come these articles never mention the possibility of the terrorist falling madly in love wanting to marry you? Anyway, I got real depressed and went to the movies. FATAL ATTRACTION. Scared the shit out of me. All those guys in the audience shouting "Kill the bitch! Kill her!" So I bet my mother a hundred bucks I'd beat the odds, and I went to work. I saw this modeling expert who said to divide my body in parts and go over it with a magnifying glass. Parts I could improve I'd work on, and the rest I'd just cover up. So I started from the top. Hair, eyebrows, cheeks, chin, nose, tits—no arms—tummy and thighs. Man, you should have seen the VISA bills.

[**JOHNNY:** Well, good for you. (*Brenda is distracted by the rest of Wanda's story.*)]

WANDA: Damn straight. I saw this modeling expert who said to divide my body in parts and go over it with a magnifying glass. Parts I could improve, I'd work on, and the rest I'd just cover up. So I started from the top. Hair, eyebrows –

[**JOHNNY:** Well, you look great. (*A Park Avenue lady sits and orders a drink.*)]

[**LADY:** Manhattan. (*Johnny makes her one. And Wanda includes her in her conversation from time to time.*)]

WANDA: [Think so?] Man, you should have seen the VISA bills. Luckily, I had a couple of boyfriends along the way who were very . . . supportive, if not marriage material. One even started to pay for my second pair of tits, but he was a recovering cocaine addict and he had a slip. And he got fired from the police department.

[(*The Park Avenue lady moves to a table.*)]

But he was very spiritual and he told me this prayer about accepting stuff I cannot change, and to just turn my breasts over to God, and God'd come up with the money for new tits.

[**JOHNNY:** "God grant me the serenity –"]

WANDA: [Right. I'll have another. (*He pours. Two 18th-century German Musketeers enter US, played by the actors who play Larry and Douglas. They groove to the music.*)] So then I went to work on my weight. I did Jenny Craig . . . Weight Watcher's, Nutrisystem, Optifast, Jenny Craig, cocaine, and finally lipo. Then I met this writer in a bar who did an article on the bet for SELF MAGAZINE, and the most beautiful thing started happening. Women all over the country started sending me donations . . .

[(*The Musketeers start singing softly in German.*)]

I got on OPRAH, Great Expectations gave me a *lifetime* membership, I even got a letter from my local councilman – it was almost like, hey, even the government wants me to win! The Kiwanis Club wants to give me their hall for my wedding. The Vanity Fair Outlet in Paramus is gonna give me a trousseau. Video Nuts is giving me and my husband a free membership, and the Taj Mahal in Atlantic City is donating the

bridal suite! So now I got thirty days to find the guy, and this morning I went to the doctor – and I got a tumor.
(*Beat; drinks.*)
And that's how I'm doing.

THE WAITING ROOM
Lisa Loomer

This is a play about power – those who have it and feel entitled, and those who don't and try to find it. Set in New York City, England, and China, in the past, present, and "both at once," three women, each from a different time and place, find themselves on common ground in the waiting room of a doctor's office. They exchange small talk, each revealing the ways she has been oppressed. Forgiveness, an 18th-century Chinese woman, has had her feet cruelly bound in order to appear helpless and attractive to her husband. Victoria, a woman from 19th-century England, is bound by both her corset and her time. She has been convinced that she must have her ovaries removed in order to cure her hysteria. Wanda, a 20th-century woman from New York, has had breast implants, lipo-suction, and facial surgery in order to beat the statistical odds and marry after the age of 35. Now her breasts have hardened and she suspects there might be more sinister complications.

Douglas, the three women's doctor, makes a desperate, emotional phone call to a fellow healer.

♦   ♦   ♦

DOUGLAS: Dr. Saganok, please, Dr. McCaskill calling and no I cannot hold . . . Good morning, doctor, you have those test results for me? . . . I see. And how was the blood work? . . . I see. And what is your recommendation? . . . WHAT!? I'm sorry, doctor, that is not an option . . . I don't care how many of these cases you've seen. I don't care if you've tried everything, try something else . . . Well, how about acupuncture? . . . Well I happen to know, it *is* being tried . . . Look, mister, you don't seem to understand what I'm saying. If it is being tried, I want to try it. I am a doctor –
(*Starts to break.*)
We don't – just – put our patients to sleep. I – my wife – we – we've had that cat for thirteen years – she, she's like our – and I can't – I just – it would break her heart – it would just shatter her heart in a thousand – . . . Don't tell me I'm getting hysterical! I'm a doctor, I can have your goddam license! I can! You're a vet, goddamit! Do something!

WHOLE HEARTED
Quincy Long

Warren is a strange and lonely man who, due to an extremely small heart, is unable to love. As a child, he killed his father, whom he hated. He meets Luisa, a Brazilian secretary. He becomes interested in her and proposes that she live with him for their mutual benefit. Later, after two farmers transplant an enormously large heart in Warren, he falls in love with Luisa.

Warren, in a straight-forward and practical manner, asks Luisa to live with him.

◆　　◆　　◆

WARREN: Listen Luisa
Upstairs
In this house
There is a bedroom
The master bedroom
That is where I would sleep
Downstairs
In the back
There is another room
A smaller room
A cozy room
It was a maid's room actually
The proportions of this room are
Well let us say that they are generous enough
The furnishings are spare
There is a toilet
And there is a view
A view of a tree as I recall
And of rolling farmland in the distance
Once or twice a week I would come down from my room and visit you in yours
You'd turn back the counterpane and we'd lay together on the iron bed
We'd press together

Hard
Like this
(*Warren squeezes his hands together and grimaces.*)
Afterwards we would walk to town
A rustic village with humble shops
Goods in the windows
Cheerful displays
Tools
Implements
Things to wear
Things to eat
Unsophisticated things that appeal to the best in us I think
You would go into the market and I would wait outside in the dark where the teenagers stand
Smoking their cigarettes and swearing
I would wait for you
We would walk home in the moonlight
I would carry the bag
The heaviness
Does this appeal to you in any way Luisa
This kind of life

WHOLE HEARTED
Quincy Long

Warren is a strange and lonely man who, due to an extremely small heart, is unable to love. As a child, he killed his father, whom he hated. He meets Luisa, a Brazilian secretary. He becomes interested in her and proposes that she live with him for their mutual benefit. Later, after two farmers transplant an enormously large heart in Warren, he falls in love with Luisa.

Jewel, Warren's childhood Nanny, tells a younger Warren a touching story about a prodigal son, hoping it will help his relationship with his father.

♦   ♦   ♦

JEWEL: Gospel say was a man
Rich man
Had him a great big business just like your daddy
Plenty of peoples workin for him
An a boy child just like you with properties and riches to have when he grow up
But this little boy he didn't want that
No
He say to his daddy
He say
Daddy
Share up your property afore you die and gimme mine
I want it
That's the way them people say in them days
And that father he done it
Why he did that way I don't know
I wouldna
So this little boy he gathered all he had and took him his journey into the city where he waste all them properties in loose livin
And when he had spent the whole damn thing up he didn't have nothin and he begun to be in serious want
So what he do but he go and join up to one of them big old

ship what go out on the ocean just like what you want to do
Oh it was cold out on that ocean
The waves was giant
Ship rollin up and down up and down
An the people's on that ship was mean an hit the boy upside his head with they big old angry fist an throw him lopside in the cabinet where they only give him rats to eat

[**YOUNG WARREN:** Rats]

JEWEL: Yeah

Rats
He eat em up too
Boy was hungry
An sick
And no one come to give him nothin else to eat an nothin for his spirit neither
Finally he up and had enough and he say to God he say God
I remember my father's people how they got food and food to spare and here I am lost out on the ocean with nothin but some rats to eat
I ever get outa here I will get my ass up and go unto my father
And I will say to him
I will say
Father
I ain't no good
My heart a mess inside a me
My heart it tiny selfish small an evil evil bad
Father
Treat me as you would one of your lowliest peoples but take me
back unto your bosom
An just as soon as them word pass out his lips them waves they quiet right down
The sun it peep out and the clouds drift out of the way
Then peoples they come unlock the door of where it is he at
An the boy squint out at them an who you s'pose his eye look up
and see

[**YOUNG WARREN:** Who]

JEWEL: His daddy

[**YOUNG WARREN:** Nooo]

JEWEL: Yeah too

His daddy was a passenger on that very ship

On his way to England to buy the richest silks an whatnots for his pretty wife

That boy he see his daddy and his daddy seen his boy and he had him great big compassions in his heart and he try to embrace his son an kiss an kiss on him like this

(*Jewel kisses Young Warren.*)

[**YOUNG WARREN:** Oooo]

JEWEL: But the son he all humble down like you doing now

He fall to his knee and say

No daddy no

I ain no good

My heart is bad with evil

I don't deserve to be your little boy

But the father say no

No

You my lovely son

An he say to his peoples that was with him he say

Bring quick the best suit I got and put it on him

Put the rings on his fingers every one

Put the two tones on his feet

Kill that fatted calf we brought for the King of England and let's eat it up and make a great big party right now

For my son he was dead and now he is alive again

He was lost and now he found

And they all sat there on that ship and had they party

That's it

That's how it was

So why you gonna circulate all over the damn world lost in somebody boat just to come an beg your daddy's forgiveness someday anyhow

You must just as well stay home

Save you all the trouble

WILD OATS
by James McLure, adapted from John O'Keefe

Described as a "Romance of the Old West," *Wild Oats* is set in the 1880's and is a comic and affectionate look at the traveling melodramas that toured the country in the late 19th century, full of cowboys, Indians, villains and bad actors. Jack Rover, an actor, impersonates a young woman's cousin and finds himself in love with her.

Here, Jack Rover describes a chaotic night where he was shot by Indians and chased by a bear.

♦ ♦ ♦

ROVER: (*A puffin' and a pantin'.*) What a night. Battling desperadoes. Getting shot in the back by Indians and pursued by a bear. How many of you folks have ever been pursued by a bear? Well, I'm here to tell ya, it was an un-bearable experience. (*Sensing the audience's hostility.*) Okay, okay. Just a little joke. He chased me for miles, folks! Chased me all night! Chased me into a box canyon. There I was trapped like a rat. The bear advanced. I could feel his hot bear breath breathing on me. Nothing more disgusting than hot bear breath. There I was. A goner. He reared up on his hind legs about to pounce. There was nothing left to do – so – I began to recite Shakespeare. At first the bear seemed curious. Puzzled, then pleased. Then actually moved. I believe I saw that beast shed a tear. Unfortunately, then I came to the line "Like to a chaos or an unlicked bear whelp." I think the bear took it personally. I know it wasn't my line reading. Anyway, the chase was on once more until as you just saw I outran him and escaped, but just barely. Thus ends a grizzly tale.

THE WOMAN WHO TRIED TO SHOUT UNDERWATER
Kelly Stuart

The Woman Who Tried to Shout Underwater is a bleak portrayal of a woman who believes she has lost everything that was important in her life. In spite of her feelings of despair and defeat, she struggles to survive. Rene, 45, has been working for a wealthy, narcissistic woman who refused to pay her. In disgust, she quits and goes to a bar to get drunk. There, she meets Chiro, a gigolo who plies her with exotic drinks, then takes her purse. Drunk and dejected, she meets Fixx, an ex-boyfriend who rejects and humiliates her further. Later, Chiro returns and tries to seduce Rene.

Here, Chiro tells Rene about an incident with on of his clients, who turns out to be Rene's former employer.

♦　♦　♦

CHIRO: (*No Accent*.) I can do English, but Italian works best. After a while it all blends in. Yesterday, this woman, she never shut up. And that's a lot of work.

Smile and smile and try to look fascinated. All I kept thinking was I wanted to leave.

We go in her bedroom and she's really noisy you know what I mean? Then her kid starts kicking on the door. Mommy Mommy I'm bleeding to death. Mommy's face goes all red. I'm the first she's had since she dumped her ex-husband. So she says in this voice – "Go play on the swing, Luanne. Go out and play on the swings." But this kid keeps screaming. . . I'm bleeding I'm bleeding. So I put on my pants and I open the door. Here's this kid with a carton full of eggs. I see her aiming right for my face. I duck, and splat, an egg hits the wall. The mother runs out and grabs the kid's toys. Throws them in the trash compactor, pushes the button. The kid just glares at me with hurt little eyes. I had to stay there. I couldn't run away. The lady's so happy to see I don't just split, that right away I can ask her for a loan. So she's getting an advance on her alimony. Maybe I could help you out in a couple of days.

THE WOMAN WHO TRIED TO
SHOUT UNDERWATER
Kelly Stuart

The Woman Who Tried to Shout Underwater is a bleak portrayal of a woman who believes she has lost everything that was important in her life. In spite of her feelings of despair and defeat, she struggles to survive. Rene, 45, has been working for a wealthy, narcissistic woman who refused to pay her. In disgust, she quits and goes to a bar to get drunk. There, she meets Chiro, a gigolo who plies her with exotic drinks, then takes her purse. Drunk and dejected, she meets Fixx, an ex-boyfriend who rejects and humiliates her further. Later, Chiro returns and tries to seduce Rene.

Rene has spurned Chiro. Alone, she recalls when her baby was taken away from her.

◆　　◆　　◆

RENE: When people are laughing I don't laugh with them.
I listen for the razor blades clicking in their throats.
Under the ocean in a cloud of raw sewage I saw
the president laughing on TV. A man was dragged
away crying and screaming as the president
laughed. The crowd broke into applause.
Everybody smiled and laughed and clapped.
If you tore away the skin I'm sure you'd find
a pair of shiny razor blades clicking together.
I don't want to go down under the water.
I don't want to stay up here with the blades. I stay in
my room where I can imagine it's raining in Hawaii and
the street is full of mud. Big fat toads are hopping in
the grass. There's a pool of cold water under the ferns.
Gecko's on the walls, parrots in the trees. And I can say
all of the filthy things I want. All the filthy filthy things.
I remember when the nurse took my baby away. There
was judgment in his eyes. He was six hours old and he knew
he'd been betrayed. Don't leave me alone in this place
he said. If you leave me alone I will never forgive you.
The nurse put her hand on my arm like this. She told me I'd

have to pull myself together. I was sobbing so loud it
embarrassed the nuns. They took me in the elevator,
told me to stop. Everything's going to be alright they said.
I went straight home and I drank champagne and
thought of my son in the big white room full of
strangers and noise, waiting for me. In the big white
room women laugh and mop the floor and he waits for
someone familiar to come. He waits like this and he listens.